## About the author

My name is Tracey-Lee Schmidt. I first started writing at the age of twelve. I grew up in a small town in South Africa. I found writing a means of expressing myself and making other people happy, using my imagination to describe different thoughts and feelings. I hope to take others on my journey of dreams.

# POETRY BOOK

# Tracey-Lee Schmidt

---

POETRY BOOK

Vanguard Press

VANGUARD PAPERBACK

© Copyright 2020
**Tracey-Lee Schmidt**

The right of Tracey-Lee Schmidt to be identified as author of
this work has been asserted by her in accordance with the
Copyright, Designs and Patents Act 1988.

**All Rights Reserved**

No reproduction, copy or transmission of this publication
may be made without written permission.
No paragraph of this publication may be reproduced,
copied or transmitted save with the written permission of the
publisher, or in accordance with the provisions
of the Copyright Act 1956 (as amended).

Any person who commits any unauthorised act in relation to
this publication may be liable to criminal
prosecution and civil claims for damages.

A CIP catalogue record for this title is
available from the British Library.

ISBN 978 1 78465 831 1

*Vanguard Press is an imprint of
Pegasus Elliot MacKenzie Publishers Ltd.*
www.pegasuspublishers.com

First Published in 2020

**Vanguard Press
Sheraton House  Castle Park
Cambridge  England**

Printed & Bound in Great Britain

# Dedication

I would like to dedicate my book to my husband, Danie Schmidt, my daughter, Stacey, and my son, Justin Dwayne. Thank you for all of your support and encouragement in putting my poetry in a book.

# Contents

13 Today ............................................................. 13
A daughter's prayer ........................................ 15
A friendly face ................................................. 17
A time and a season ........................................ 18
Being born ........................................................ 21
Chaffe in the wind ........................................... 23
Chains ............................................................... 25
Dad .................................................................... 26
Hearts beat as one ........................................... 27
Hold on tight .................................................... 29
Hope .................................................................. 30
Inner Strength ................................................. 31
Mothers ............................................................. 32
My Heart ........................................................... 34
Nature ............................................................... 35
Peace ................................................................. 37
Raging earth ..................................................... 38
Rare gems ......................................................... 39
Slipping away ................................................... 40
Small town dreams ......................................... 43

The heart of a mother ............................................ 46
The Jester ............................................................. 48
Wishes .................................................................. 49
Woman ................................................................. 50

## 13 Today

For you,
this is just another day.
Maybe embarrassing now,
this day you will look back on.
To me,
your mother.
I know and hear you say,
"Come on mom, get over it."
That way you shake your head,
give me that side long glance,
roll of your eyes.
My boy,
now it's my chance.
From teethers to rattles,
from teddies to girls.
Go on,
shake your head,
I've seen it all.
Okay, okay, I'll give you a break.
One more thing…
Your voice might break,
you'll grow a beard.
I know that now,

that sounds pretty weird.
All too soon,

you'll want to drive my car.
Hold on,
slam on those brakes.
Until that day arrives,
the car is mine.
For now,
just stay as you are.
Enjoy your friends,
make the most of it.
Most important,
be proud to be you.

# A daughter's prayer

When I wake in the morning,
While the day is still dawning.
I get down on my knees,
say a little prayer.

Dear Father up above,
who looks on us with love.
I pray send an angel,
to watch over my mom.

Lord, I thank you for her love,
each and every day.
When I reach out,
she is there.

Lord Jesus,
You gave me a mom who cares.
Thank you for her endless love,
sent from up above.

Thank you Lord,
as I grew up.
You gave me a mom,
who loves.

My prayer to you this day,
let her know she is loved.
Send her some warm,
happy thoughts.

Thank you Lord for her, an angel in disguise.
For the love in her heart,
the sunshine in her eyes.


Each and every day,
let her know I care.
even though far away,
I keep her close to my heart.

# A friendly face

A friendly face,
I see in you.
Each day as I pass on by.
I thank God up above
for creating love,

Without it we wouldn't last.
With a wave of your hand
the way you say "Hello",
I see your friendliness show.

Stay as you are,
don't change a thing.
You are a blessing to all,
who come to stay.
With sadness I say goodbye.
With a happy heart to know,
your friendly face will be here,
when next we visit,
or come to stay.

## A time and a season

I came into this circle,
so snug and tight.
Not knowing if I would fit
or whether the fit felt just right.

At first it was a battle, a battle I fought inside.
The tiny voice inside me,
roaring in my ears.

Telling me to run,
run for my life.
See, this is what I had always done,
instead of running I decided to stay.
I had done enough running,
I just wanted the pain to go away.

After every single hurt,
my heart in two would rip.

I watched from a distance,
a fight still inside.
A nudging voice I could hear,
give me a chance, let me draw you near.

Slowly things began to change,
I was feeling braver.

More alive on the inside
With each word that was spoken by each of you here,
Each time a stitch was sewing up my heart.
I'm no longer alone,
no longer bound by fear.
Fear of what everyone would think,
I was mending and I had friends to lean on.

For this reason I stand before you today,
heart and feelings exposed.
I found my place and the fit is snug,
a piece of a puzzle joining to form one.

If I could give any advice,
it would be to hang on tight.
Strap yourself in,
for the greatest ride of your life.

God has not forgotten you,
he made you to fit in.

Come in closer,
come in and sit.


Look at the person,
sitting at your side.
We are all here for one or other reason,

Just remember,
this could be your season.

Thank God for bringing us all together,
you are each in your own way,
wonderfully formed and unique,
together we make the most beautiful
flower collection,
brought here by God.

# Being born

On the day,
that you were born.
I could have sworn,
I saw angels above your bed.
Smiles on their faces,
tears in their eyes.
Crying tears,
cause they were losing an angel.
The smiles of all the joy,
you'd give us just being you.
You are evidence,
evidence of love,
your dad's and mine.
Watching you grow,
over the years.
Through both smiles
sometimes a tear.
From that little baby,
we took home.
To the lovely girl,
you have become.
Know this,
Those angels are still with you.

Each and every day you open your eyes,

they watch over you.
You are our precious daughter,
our, little angel.

## Chaffe in the wind

It's the change of season
Green grass changing to brittle brown
Easy to bend
Easy to break
Ever so feathery as it crushes in your hands
Hold it up blow away the flakes
Watch them blowing to and fro
The heart of it has been crushed
Blown in all directions
Trampled upon
Matted in hair
Drifting down a stream
Our life is much like this
One minute we are strong
Nothing can break us
One harsh word
One hurt feeling
The heart crushed
Trampled beyond repair
Emotions blown in all directions
The only way to make it whole is to give it to God He
can restore what others have broken
Time to heal
Time to feel
Feel whole and worthy

Not pushed aside and discarded
We are all created by God
We all deserve to live
To be treated with respect
By gentleness
Forgive those people
People who threw you aside
No thoughts for your feelings
No thoughts how you broke and cried
Let go of the pain

# Chains

By earthly chains
We feel bound
Trying to hold us back
Holding us down
Our God our Father
Has given us the key
In his word it says
He came to set the captives free
Furthermore his word states
In Isaiah 53: 5
By his stripes we are healed
This is there for you and for me
We should not accept defeat
 His forgiveness
He gives
Feel his love
It courses in us all
As does his life giving blood
Remember always
He died for you and me
All because of this
We!
Are set apart for  him.

# Dad

All day I sat and racked my brains,
for the perfect gift.
A gift befit,
to give your heart a lift.
maybe a bunny girl dressed in pink,
seeing to your every whim.
Then I remembered your blood pressure,
I abandoned that thought immediately.
You need something better,
something to cherish,
to make you feel better.
My words to you today are these,
you are the greatest dad by far.
I may be able to recite you this poem,
remind you that you're never alone.
These words I write sincerely
take care of your wonderful heart.
Take these words,
hold them close.
Remember this,
we are only a heartbeat away.

## Hearts beat as one

Flutter, flutter, feel me shudder
Whenever you are near
My feet are light
My heart takes flight
Emotions in a turmoil.
I gaze into your eyes
I can't disguise
All these feelings deep inside
Take my hand,
Hold me close
Never let me go.
Together we walk
No need for talk
Our hearts beating as one.
Brought together,
By the hands of God,
You hold the keys to my heart.
These things are certain
I can honestly say,
Each and every day.
My love for you
Will never change.
Each day I kneel,
To God I pray.
Our love will only deepen
As time goes by

With a satisfied sigh.
Standing as one together
Our hearts, still beat as one…

# Hold on tight

Thump, thump,
Thump, thump,
Sounds of my heart
Beating to a drum
Hand to my chest
Beating so hard
All else silent
I feel as though I'm spinning
Teetering to one side
I fear if I let go
All will drop
The fear in me tightens
Beads of sweat on my skin
When will the spinning end?
Clutching my chest
Breathing slowing down
I fall on my knees to the ground
Slowly things come into focus
I never know
When it will strike again?
For just a while
My world feels normal.

# Hope

In a meadow stood a mighty Oak,
awaiting its time to be spoke.
Upon its branches strong and wide,
there grew seeds awaiting the tide.
"What tide is this?" I hear you ask,
It's the one that comes by the hand of the Lord. All of
a sudden the seeds released,
some to the west others to the east.
One particular seed most unfortunate,
fell among weeds to its misfortune.
The Lord looked down upon this seed,
he lifted it out from amongst the seeds.
"Listen little seed," said the Lord,
"although small your potential is great.
Take your place under my wing,
For you it's never too late."
To this the seed replied,
"To the world I'm nothing but a dismal seed"
To this the Lord answered,
"Faith my little seed is all you need,
To spread your wings and do mighty things." Upon
hearing this he knew he could grow,
Into a mighty oak ready to sow.
He would stand witness to all other seeds,
for he had faith to do great deeds.

## Inner Strength

I go with you
Wherever you are
For we carry each other
In our hearts
In my thoughts
You will constantly be
Our love is strong
It survives obstacles
It stays strong in the storms
Our roots are intertwined
This is the reason we stand strong
When the going gets tough.
Although the road has its bends
With our love
It cannot contend
Like a flowing river
That stays the course
Together we stand
A strong force.

# Mothers

This is for all mothers out there,
mothers old and new.
In remembrance of mothers lost,
mothers with us today.
This is for you,
Thank-you for every day.
First a word of warning,
to each person here.
A life given,
can also be taken away.
Take a second,
Look around,
there's a mother to be found.
Take your mother,
hold her near,
She is the one who wipes away a tear.
She held you close,
Rocked you to sleep at night.
Stood vigil at your bedside,
set the bogeyman to take flight.
While you were asleep,
lost in dreamland,
she tiptoed in,
to hold your hand.
She comforted you,
when you fell and scraped your knee.

When first love comes around,
a mother will always be found.
Mothers are always around,
to give words of wisdom.
A shoulder to cry on,
an ear to listen.
Don't question how,
Don't question why?
The list is endless,
I could go on and on.
Take a second,
take a minute to reflect on life,
Thank your Mom for being in it.
Give her that chance,
Get to know her.
Listen when she speaks,
don't brush her away.
Tell her she's great,
tell her you care,
She might not always be there.
Regrets come fast,
far too late.
Seize the moment,
while she is around.
Take a moment,
thank her for always being there.

# My Heart

My heart it aches
My heart it breaks
Knowing you're so far away
I can't reach out just a touch
Just one touch wouldn't be enough
I need more
So much more
I need your arms wrapped around me
Your tender kiss
On my lips
With each minute
Each hour
Each day
I'm counting the seconds
As they tick away
I'm waiting eagerly for your return
My heart it longingly yearns
For when you come back
My heart hurts
My eyes too
All of the crying without you
Hurry home my love
To where you belong
Safely wrapped in my arms I love you my honey
With all my heart

# Nature

Sitting in the throes of nature,
God's presence all around.
Watching every creature,
with each a unique sound.
Bursting forth,
from every flower,
a glorious burst of color.
Close your eyes,
let your senses come alive.
From the clouds above,
to the grass beneath your feet.
God the creator,
gave us all of these.
I watch a little bird,
as it hops on closer.
Curiosity in its eyes,
for just that second.
I hold my breath,
a tilt of his head,
shake of his wings,
before he takes flight.
I feel the breeze,
gentle against my skin.
Calming me from within.
At one with nature,

I calmly sit.
Taking pleasure,
in all Gods gifts.

# Peace

Seated here,
on this bench.
I feel at last,
peace within.
With each deep breath,
I seem to take.
My soul becomes calm,
my heartbeat slows,
twirling with the breeze,
brushing against my skin.
My head turned up,
I gaze upon the skies.
I look at things,
through different eyes.
At that moment,
one with nature,
My senses come alive.
Through the songs of the birds,
carried on the breeze,
I hear God whisper to me.
Fingers of sunshine,
touch my skin.
Slowly a healing,
from within.
I know through God.
I can live again.

# Raging earth

Destruction…despair
Nature in dis-repair
Waters churning
Anger in its depths
Humankind stop and stare
Remorse….regret
Feelings in a turmoil
Nature fighting back
Trees and man become one
As raging waters rage attack
Did we ignore earths cry for help?
It shook and shuddered beneath our feet
Life went on
No defeat
In the blink of an eye
Waters rise
Cries for help
Heave sighs
Should we have noticed…
Earth's demise…?

# Rare gems

You're the twinkle in the sky,
Before I go to bed at night.
The moonbeam,
Shining through my window.
It softly touches my skin,
Soft and gentle as the flutter of butterflies wings.
When you fold me in your arms,
I feel safe and warm.
It takes me back to my childhood,
When I fell and scraped my knee.
The tenderness and love,
You lift me up.
Brush away my tears and fears.
As I grew older,
That love never changed
Even though,
I was growing into a woman.
Your love and tenderness,
Remained the same.
To me,
You are as a pure gem.
Cradled in the softest of velvet,
Not to be harmed.
Today and forever,

The greatest gift…a mother's love.

## Slipping away

Life is ebbing,
slipping away.
Like sand in an hourglass, time it slips,
Slips away day by day.

Robbing us of everything precious,
like running water,
Slipping through our veins.
What is life,
if no-one cares

Never standing still,
leaving lifelessness in its wake.
A loss of own,
This holds us down.
I feel life ebbing,
ebbing away.
Tiredness enveloping me,
dragging me slowly slowly away
tired of obstacles always in my way.

I sit and huddle,
knees under chin.
Tears silently run down my cheeks,
I'm tired, I'm exhausted
I want to give in.

I look to the heavens,
I stretch out my hands in desperation.
From deep inside,
a strangled cry.
Help me, Father,
I don't know how.
My head on my knees,
still hurting still tired.

In this time I don't see the light,
it shines bright enveloping me all around.
Inch by inch I lift my head,
the light's so bright
I need to shield my eyes.

I hear a voice calling my name
My child, my chosen,
Look at me, I'm here to set you free,
I open my eyes and look around.

I'm overwhelmed by the warmth of love,
a love like no other.
I'm lifted gently,
by hands unseen

so soft so gentle so warm.
I look towards the obstacles before me,
look my child, I never left your side.

I walked tentatively forward stepping in faith,
as Peter walked on the water .

Obstacles in my path seemed to grow smaller, only by facing them
Dealing with them
Only then can they become this way.

I look to the heavens once again,
I cry out to my Father
Lord grant me the strength,
renew my energy
knowing my Father God never leaves my side
I can conquer anything trying to knock me down don't lose sight,
Don't ever doubt.
God's always with us,
it's only in our own human flesh
that's when we feel he has left.
God, never leaves.

## Small town dreams

I had a dream
I'd one day change destiny
Take control of my own fate.
Unfortunately that wasn't what
Destiny had in mind for me.

I was a small town girl
With small time dreams.
Somehow that life
Came apart at the seams.

I felt I was drowning
My dreams were drowning too.
Growing up in a small town
Along with my small time dreams.

I had a very real need
To get out amongst the weeds.
To plant a pretty garden
A garden of dreams.

I wasn't my own
Until from the nest I had flown.
Leaving behind
That small, small town.

My dreams
No longer small time dreams .
I finally had got rid of those weeds
I started planting my own pretty seeds.

I finally found I could breathe
In my garden void of weeds.
I take a breath
I look around.

Oh what joy
Oh what peace.
The wind in my hair
Feel of grass beneath my feet.

Surrounded by my beautiful flowers
Beneath the branches of a strong oak tree.
I had finally found a place
I could just be me.

This strong oak
Had a place in my heart.
This life our life
Our seeds became flowers
Strong and unique.

The passion of that small town girl
Grew stronger each day.
No longer just dreams

It had become my reality.
We all deserve happiness
We all deserve to dream.

# The heart of a mother

Nobody understands the heart of a mother
Only the heart of another mother
Knowing what sacrifices she makes
I know because those sacrifices were made for me The unconditional love
No strings attached
I know I was born out of love
Not under contract
Who can understand the excitement?
Holding your child's hand
On their first day of school
Me cause you were holding mine
Knowing the satisfaction
When your child succeeds
I know this
Your love shines through your smiles
What it feels like when your child falls
I know this
You were there to pick me up
To go through labor pains
Knowing it's all forgotten
With that first smile
You knew one day love would come my way.
Watching your daughter walk down the aisle
Your cheeks wet with joy
No…you are right

I don't know how that feels
There is one thing I do know for sure
You did succeed.

# The Jester

Once upon a time,
I was needed far and wide.
Going around telling my stories,
in drama or in mime.
I would travel from country to country,
putting smiles on all faces.
crossing many rivers and boundaries,
leaving a trail of laughter behind.
Lords and ladies,
Kings and queens.
Sent for me.
Entertainment for parties.
leaving sighs of astonishment,
giggles all around.
My acting and characters,
almost real
Yes, I was a court jester,
trained to make people laugh.
My trade was very popular,
amongst all noblemen across the land.

# Wishes

If I were a sprite,
In this dark and blackened night.
I'd walk across a moonbeam,
pluck a star from the sky.
First I would sit right down,
just gaze upon the moon.
It is truly,
a magnificent sight.
Perfectly positioned,
surrounded by a halo of light.
On a clear and cloudless night,
reaching across the earth.
Bathing all it touches,
in glorious delight.
If I close my eyes,
stretch out my hand.
For a moment becoming part of me,
And I of it.
For the briefest of moments,
I'm frozen in time.
Gazing around,
the world rushes by.
Stop…wait,
Can you not see?
the moon is there,
for both you and me.

# Woman

Being a women
Being a mom
All comes with changes
Its part of our life
Being a women
Being a wife
This my friends
A change of life
You run around in a frazzle
You give up your makeup
You end up in tracksuits
And a ponytail
Not quite a mess
Just a back seat
You realize after years
Maybe you let go
Let yourself slip
You no longer
Seem to be hip
You traded your looks
For glasses and books
Despite these changes
You have what it takes
Hey ladies
Take another look
From cinders

To ball gown
You still have it all
Yes, life changes
It's not a bad thing
After all
It's just a little bling
You gave your heart
You made a start
Yes there will be mountains to climb
Puddles you trip through
Through all this
We agree
Compared to the world
And all its chaos
We still come out on top
All of us women
Great things in common
God is in charge
He gave us life
Who of us here
Could ask for a better life

www.ingramcontent.com/pod-product-compliance
Lightning Source LLC
LaVergne TN
LVHW041550060526
838200LV00037B/1223